Night of the Blue Moon
Jazz Poems & Stories

By
Beverly Welch

PublishAmerica
Baltimore

© 2009 by Beverly Welch.
All rights reserved. No part of this book may be reproduced, stored in a retrieval system or transmitted in any form or by any means without the prior written permission of the publishers, except by a reviewer who may quote brief passages in a review to be printed in a newspaper, magazine or journal.

First printing

PublishAmerica has allowed this work to remain exactly as the author intended, verbatim, without editorial input.

ISBN: 1-60703-670-3
PUBLISHED BY PUBLISHAMERICA, LLLP
www.publishamerica.com
Baltimore

Printed in the United States of America

Dedication

These poems and stories are dedicated to
Daniel S. Welch
musician, artist, husband, father, grandfather and friend
gathered to his ancestors
April 23, 1989

May you be free.
May you be happy.
May you be at peace.
May you be at rest.
May you know we remember you.
May you know we love you.

Acknowledgments

I give thanks to jazz and all those who make it.
I also want to thank its aficionados,
especially Richard Parker and Wendell Patrick, Sr.,
who encouraged me to make poems and stories
in praise of it

Introduction

Jazz has been an inspiration for me since I was a child and danced to Woody Herman's "Apple Honey" with my father in our kitchen.

Radio shows like Leigh Kammon's "Jazz Image" and Dick Landfield's "Night Flight" introduced me to bop, bossa nova and Miles' "Birth of the Cool". Ken Nordine's "Word Jazz" and Jack Kerouac's "On the Road" taught me music's relationship to the literary arts of poetry and story.

This collection of poems and stories was written over a period of twenty years and reflects music I have heard in neighborhood clubs, concert halls, and parks, in the cities of Minneapolis, St. Paul, New Orleans, Seattle, Havana and Paris and on the radio, vinyl, taped cassette and CD.

The poems and stories pay tribute to jazz, its players and also to its many "char-actors" (thank you, Dr. John) who inhabit the jazz world.

Wynton Marsalis has said that jazz, and the way it is played, can be used as a model for modern society. As he explains it, each musician expresses him/her self in a solo and finally, all the musicians come together in harmony.

May these poems and stories contribute to that harmony.

Jazz in the Park

Jerry Gonzales and the Fort Apache Band
playing bop,
wild and free into the wind.
The smells of corn popping and
coffee brewing
mingle with earth smells
of grass,
newly sprouted leaves;
damp soil.
People gather
sitting on blankets and benches and
on the grass.
Children dance,
creating their own styles,
into the music;
digging it;
feeling it;
wanting more.
The sun begins its descent
on the western horizon.
The coolness of the night
accepts the melodies,
the popcorn and coffee smells,
the damp earth,
new leaves

and dancing children
like an
evening prayer
(a homage to the day).
The Fort Apache Band plays
their last tune,
a sermon in praise
to the coming night.

The Jazz Men

They took the bandstand, all in black, three-button suits,
narrow black ties, neat against white starched shirt fronts;
soft-spoken men with neatly cut hair, clean shaven
wearing horn-or black-rimmed glasses.
We came in between sets and they were sitting at tables,
sipping espresso, puffing on meerschaum pipes filled with cherry blend
tobacco.
The smoke from their pipes drifted into the light in blue trails.
After a time, the four varied shades of brown-skinned men
took the bandstand again.
The drummer, sitting on a stool behind his instruments,
unbuttoned his coat and, picking up his brushes,
made a few playful swipes at his cymbals
while smiling at a girl sitting down front.
The piano player unbuttoned his coat too and sat down
while the bass player picked up his big upright
and the tenor man picked up his horn.
They began to play and the notes slid over the piano keys
and bass strings and drums
producing intelligent melodies
that got inside our heads
and made us know we were hearing truth for the first time.
And the golden saxophone played New York, Chicago
and Kansas City notes, making us feel the joy of love
and the sorrow in leaving.

We understood the dark nights of slaves
and the humiliation of Jim Crow
and believed we were now standing in the noontime
of some new and splendid beginning
given to us by these men—
these prophets, preaching the gospel of jazz.

Royal Suite

The Duke
Swept into the elegant magic
of "Such Sweet Thunder,"
we danced inside haunted melodies
in the midnight hour
of a soft, spring night
where the Duke of Ellington
was loving us
madly.

The Count
Regal man, Count Basie
sitting at his piano,
giving the downbeat
in his inimitable way
and then,
that big band machine
of brass and rhythm
began to play "Silk Shiny Stockings"
and men and women
took the floor,
grooving with their bodies;
lost in the rhythms of dance;
amazed at their grace;
obeying the Count's
Royal Command.

Night Song

She is a wild song
singing in the night;
a honey-colored woman
with tarnished, gold hair
wearing red high heels;
sipping pink champagne
dancing like a puppet
on the string of illusion.

Women on the Avenue
Women in high heels
and black panty hose
"dip" in conversations
all along the avenue,
doing their best;
learning to be ladies
from queens.

Night of the Blue Moon

She was made of golden light and at the right time of day, you could look straight through her. He was made of bronze and red flames smoldering low, except for a certain time at night.

They stayed together in a small room which was their point of departure for intergalactic travel on cold, crystal nights.

They were amused by the men and woman of the planet as they danced among them, swirling, leaping and circling just out of reach; an uncrowned king and queen, unrecognized with no titles, except for those who knew them and loved and hated them all at once.

Her job had always been trying to fit in while his had always been not to.

Their refrigerator contained champagne and Cuban cigars which they sipped and he smoked. Her secret stash of cigarettes was smoked by her alone because he thought they might make her die, even though she knew she would die from dancing too long to the sweet jazz music in too many early dawns.

When they were not together, they worked jobs, paid rent and walked alone past silent storefronts. He cooked real meals while she ate things from boxes, cartons and cans. She prayed in church while he played gentlemen's games with men who weren't. They watched movies and appeared separately at social functions, smiling, nodding and making conversations with men and women and children who sensed the secret they shared and wanted to be included.

Sometimes, they were afraid because they had forgotten where they were from and why they had been brought together.

He had been cast out from a place stone cold with screaming, where life was gone in a flash of fire in the midst of broken glass and back doors; a place where herbs given by the gods were refined by demons in incense-filled rooms by lost angels and spoiled warriors. He was cast out into silent darkness, leaving flesh and bones and muscle behind until he became a secret fire glowing in the emptiness.

She was cast out of a sterile yet putrid smelling room filled with dying men and women into the space beyond till she was only a strange, sweet perfume traveling on the wind.

Then there was a silent time of peace with only dark, soft winds to ride upon.

Each arrived to a separate, cold winter place, shocked and shivering after their journey through the quiet.

The snow surrounding her glittered with diamond ice and the granite buildings surrounding him, reflected cold hearts in their windows. Animals sniffed her with their frosty breath and walked away. Men and women, their heads bent against the wind, took no notice of him.

Couples (men and women this world calls parents) took them to their separate houses in their separate places to teach, trick and tame them, or so they thought. Because inside each of them was a longing for something lost.

So, they looked and listened inside the mornings along roads and streets. Bright noontimes found them waiting in dusty schools and dim churches. They visited noisy bars and silent museums and walked on moonlit beaches alone and separate from the night. They wandered down bright hospital corridors and caught the stars and moon in their hands through prison bars. All the while, melancholy songs were singing in their hearts.

Then, one night under the second full moon of the first month of a new year, they met and the secret was there between them, too bright to see, too light to touch, but there all the same.

While they searched and stumbled and tested each other, the secret they remembered hovered just out of reach, dazzling them with its presence, wrapping itself around them with its magic mantle when they were apart.

Even then, fear and doubt sometimes filled their hearts and the sad songs inside them starting singing again.

Finally, they reached out and took what had always been theirs. The secret settled upon them and in them; their eyes and skin and hair glowed with its magnificent magic and it was theirs to keep forever.

Remembering Miles & Saint John

Miles,
fighting the bull
one last time
in Montreaux
and
blowing him away
with
"Sketches of Spain".
Saint John Coltrane,
playing for God,
past sorrow and joy.
Further out.
Sheets of sound
EXPLODING
somewhere
in the galaxy.

Poem for Oscar

Oscar's melodies
    Skip
Over
    The
        Keys
Like childhood memories
Of school's
    Last day.

Glass Heart

He came to me
out of the rain
naked, except for his clothes;
limping, slightly wounded
from old wars.
His heart was a white diamond,
bright and multi-faceted
glimmering in his chest.
Later I discovered
it was only glass.

Shatterlee

He was all broken inside
although
on the outside he looked
perfectly good.
But when he talked
it was easy to tell
he had shattered parts.
And when he walked,
you could clearly see him
fading away.

Remembering Thelonious Sphere Monk

Thelonious Sphere Monk,
making it in a
minor key,
so awesome and strange
it made us afraid
we would be lost
in some mysterious place
we were afraid
to go.
Monk,
giving us his version of living,
"Straight: No Chaser."

Love Story in Blue

The spring in which they met was deep blue with thunder. When they whispered and kissed in taxicabs, it was behind rain streaked windows.

No wonder that when he painted the milky, white likeness of her Scandinavian flesh, he placed a flash of lightning on the canvas which split her body in two. She also had no head in the painting and her arms were like wings carrying the two halves of her through space.

Critics saw the work as revolutionary and claimed it black with explanations beyond the artist's intention. He chose to make no comment and hid behind the angry darkness of his skin.

The model accepted her notoriety without quotation as well, which only added elements of mystery and sparked further speculation in the daily news. Artist's and model's reputation grew, and they became more and more sought after in their milieu.

She modeled for him alone and further paintings seemed to verify the critics' interpretations of the artist's anger and its explosive expression on canvas. Politicians commented on his daring, which amused the artist and his subject, as they enjoyed the luxury fame brought them in the solitary confinement of their love.

They walked in the park near their apartment at odd hours. Early morning joggers or late night hustlers paid them no mind as artist and model strolled hand in hand.

"Would you ever marry me?" she inquired.

"Never," he said.

"Will you have my baby?" he questioned.

"Never," she replied.

Jazz Ballet

I used to write
      Jazz ballets in the air
(And watch them dance there.)
Ladies/bright; dressed in light
Dancing with
Coffee-colored gentlemen in clothes
Of smoke.
Smoke circling light…
      Up,
            Over,
                  Beyond,
And through.
Smoke and light in the night
Dancing
      "sorta blue"

Café de la Huchette
Le Célèbre Temple du Jazz

Chaque soir un orchestra de jazz
pour le plaisir d'ecouter
ou de danser
dans la plus pure tradition
avec les meilleurs bopeurs
de paris
de club evoque
de la grande époque
du Cotton Club et du Savoy*
*Every evening a jazz band
For listening pleasure
Or to dance
In timeless tradition
With the best boppers
Of Paris
The club remembers
The Cotton Club and the Savoy

Then and There

Miles Davis...
Always moving on and on
and on,
talking way "up in there"
in a hushed, cool
whisper,
so still;
so quiet;
to make you stop
and listen,
like,
when you first heard
his horn,
you HAD to
stop
and stay
in that sweet, sad, cool
Then and There.
Billie Holiday...
with a sanctified face
ravaged by junk,
sang melancholy songs
from her bleeding soul
and kept us spellbound
in the instant of

her suffering.
Stan Getz…
tenor man,
lives in playful riffs
of summertime sambas
forever
on taped cassettes
of frozen moments.
Miles, Billie and Getz…
all sleeping now
in peaceful,
evil silence.

Left Bank of the World
(Ode for Two Chets)

"He passed gently," they said;
"with grace,
Élan. He took a long time to die…"
Their voices trailed off.
You kept my letters
tied in bundles;
marked in years,
and so,
I was always at your side,
long ago;
then,
      and now,
On the Left Bank of the World.
We sip cognac from your silver flask at first light.
I place my cigarette in its long holder and
lean toward you for a light.
Your sunglasses hide the blue in your eyes.
Your hair brushes the collar
of your careless shirt.

I take a drag from my cigarette and
exhale its smoke in exquisite rings.
I kiss your effete, "white" lips.
You say, "I love you" in aristocratic,

tender tones.

On the Left Bank of the World,

somewhere in the shadows,

the other Chet picks up his horn

and plays an understated,

hip melody.

For you;

for him;

      for me.

Seattle Scene

Railroad men who worked on the old Empire Builder that ran between Chicago and Seattle liked to tell stories about that Northwestern city before it became "sanitized and computerized". They remembered hearing that an outfit called Boeing was making an airplane that flew without propellers and used jet propulsion instead. They told stories of pawn shops, blues and jazz bars and sailors and their women and drinking and dancing with them all along the waterfront of Elliott Bay.

Seattle was the city to which Kerouac returned after serving as a fire watchman on Desolation Peak. The experience inspired his novel, "Desolation Angels". It is the city where Quincy Jones and Ray Charles birthed their music and where "Holy" Hendrix honed guitar chops to speak for his generation. The great jazz and blues singer, Joe Williams sang his last song there.

The waterfront is now filled with condos and hotels; restaurants and souvenir shops catering to tourists. Boats line the piers waiting to show visitors around the bay. Pioneer Square and Skid Row are sanitized too, although a few homeless men and women hang around on park benches until they are tracked down by cell-phone wielding social workers.

Bud's Record Shop remains. It is a place still offering vinyl records alongside more modern versions of recorded music. You can find long-ago recorded songs by Q, Brother Ray and Joe Williams along with copies of the Hendrix "Experience". The store is in a basement and it's okay to linger, ask questions and talk awhile about the music.

There are street musicians, playing all kinds of music, at the Public Market and just up the hill from it at Post Alley. Around the corner, there is a Marxist book store offering leftist posters, Free Mumia buttons and the writing of Franz Fanon and Malcolm X. Small restaurants offer foods from many cultures and the odor of garlic and curry mingles with the smell of fresh brewed coffee.

Up on Capitol Hill there are stories on the wind and mysteries to probe. You can visit the graves of Bruce Lee and his son and hope their warrior spirits might somehow enter your being. At the same time, you pray the curse that killed them is nowhere near. Or you can bus out to Fremont and visit the troll under the bridge. Fremont, its inhabitants claim, is the center of the universe.

The city is named after the Suquamish Chief, Seattle. Many environmentalists see him as a saint of sorts who watches over the mountains, forests and streams. Perhaps he is just that. Maybe he resides along with other saints and deities on Mount Rainer, that beautiful, majestic volcanic mountain that watches over the city season after season. Perhaps the mountain waits until the day it will have had enough and decides to erupt in a magnificent explosion that may be a final sign to the North American continent.

Sometimes

Will you think about me
in the "sometimes"
of another day?
After you have kissed me
that last time,
will you wonder
where I am?
        And
(like the song)
"wonder who's kissing me now"?
Will you miss me
when you remember
the laughing and loving
and how we thought we were
SOMETHING?

Blues in Autumn

Did the blues begin in autumn
with a blaze of red rust
and golden dust
      scattered
on concrete and brick?
Or did they start
in wavering reflections
of neon lights
and street lamps
      shimmering
on pavement?
Were they already singing
in a September morning
haunted
by summer's mist?
I hear the rust
and gold dust
refined in smoke,
in the blazing, shimmering,
wavering voices
of "melancholy babies"
in bars along city avenues.
They sing summer's end':
Moaning,
Whispering,
"Blues
in the night".

Time

Time stands still.
It also races
and slips away.
Convicts do time;
Men make time;
Couples spend time.
People say they had a
good time or
a sad or bad time.
Drummers keep time
and
there are those who
kill time
and others who
measure it.

But,
does anybody know
What time it is?

Silly Blues

My eye is blue.
The sky is blue.
Am I blue?
Blue nude;
Blue mood;
Cool blue;
New blue;
Silly blues.

Variation on Miss Otis Regrets

I've marked the box "cannot attend"
on my invitation to the Ball.
I'll wear no sequined gown
and instead content myself with a
simple dress in black;
widow's weeds
to mourn sorrows deeply mysterious
and complicated.
Tonight I'll seat myself at a table
for one, fingering
an empty dance card signed
with regrets.
I'll receive no guests and be
unable to see you today or
even sometime soon.
Clouds, heavy with sorrowful snow,
lie low over the city.
Costumed children honor All Saints.
Let the dead rest
and let me remember and then
forget

Gentle breezes touching their hair;
eyes squinting against the sun;
laughter gone silent;

blackbirds singing outside a room
filled with the stench of decayed flesh.
Let me remember and then
forget:
A child-sized coffin,
white with innocent longing
for angel song;
a note saying "goodbye"
that left
no forwarding address.
My mailbox overflows with gentle intentions,
invitations and messages begging
urgent reply. I send my regrets:
Unable to lunch today.

Here & Now

The jazz men,
Working day jobs
To please their women
And feed their kids,
Sort mail,
Build houses,
And counsel and doctor and teach
While the jazz light shines
All day in their brains
As they create
And syncopate,
And everything
All the time
Is improvised
To become
One
Big, beautiful, long
Jazz song.

Aventura en Cuba
(Adventure in Cuba)

I arrived in Havana, Cuba via Gulfstream International Airlines on a Saturday in mid-July of 2005. My companions and I were part of a mission group traveling on a special visa. Our arrival coincided with the aftermath of Hurricane Dennis, which hit Cuba fairly hard. Consequently, when we arrived there was no electric power except at the airport, in hospitals and at certain hotels with their own generators. As we drove into Havana from Jose Marti Airport, soldiers were checking neighborhoods to make sure citizens were safe. Our Cuban hosts decided we were typical "crazy North Americans" and named our decision to fly "reckless". I couldn't help but agree. When we reached the church dormitory that was to be our home for the next several days, the first thing I noticed was "a kiss from the breeze that awakens you." (Fernan Sanchez) There is something about a tropical breeze that wraps itself around you and stays on your skin.

Sometime during the night, electric power was restored, because when a rooster's crow awakened me, I noticed ceiling fans whirring above me. Though not good by American standards, there was enough water pressure for brushing of teeth and a quick shower. I was the first one of the women in our group to awaken. Perhaps this is because I am the only one who smokes and craved my first cigarette of the day. Stepping outside, I was surrounded by the lushness of tropical trees, plants, flowers and birds and the antiquity of centuries-old houses. The rest of my group soon joined me in the dining hall where an excellent chef, had prepared a tasty breakfast of eggs, cheese, bread, fresh mangoes and rich coffee.

Following breakfast, we went to church where we were welcomed by the Cuban congregation. As part of the service, we asked God's blessing for President Castro. Worship over, discussion about how it felt, as Americans, to ask that Fidel Castro find favor in God's eyes ensued. Opinions varied.

Part of the reason for our journey was indeed to unite as brothers and sisters in faith with Cubans and another was to provide some assistance with needed work around the church including some painting and gardening. Beginning on Monday, we worked mornings, before the heat of the day took hold. I spent most afternoons helping prepare our evening meal, sitting with Cuban women in the courtyard peeling, cutting and chopping yucca, onions and garlic speaking to each other in halting Spanish and English punctuated with many gestures meant to improve communication.

Supper preparations complete, we walked through the neighborhood, visiting with older Cuban women who lived at "The House of Grandmothers" or Cuban men and women refreshing themselves with Havana Club coolers at the local bodega. Cubans seemed eager and unafraid to talk with us. When they found we were from Minnesota, a typical first response was, "Minnesota Twins! Tony Oliva!" The Cubans continue to love baseball as much as in Hemmingway's day and have great pride in Oliva and other Cuban-born players who played or play in the U.S.

On one such afternoon, more serious discussion took place. "I do not," one man declared, "work for a dictator. I work for the people, especially for the young and for the old." He went on to speak of his admiration for President Castro's intelligence and told us he was proud of Cuba's healthcare and education systems. "Our doctors," he said, "train health care workers throughout Africa and Latin America. Our education is free to everyone."

These sentiments were echoed by many Cubans with whom I spoke, but there were jokes too. The one most commonly heard that summer, the 46th Anniversary of the Revolution, was that "Fidel Castro has been President for 46 years and still had not learned how to make a 'Cuba Libre' (a common Cuban drink consisting of rum & coke). Cuba Libre' literally means "a free Cuba".

A highlight in Havana included visits to La Zorra El Ceurvo (The Vixen and the Crow) one of the world's renowned jazz clubs. Gilberto Valdez, a great Cuban drummer explained to me that he loved to play with North American jazz players. I asked him if he would like to live in the USA. "No," he replied. "The money there gets in the way of creative playing."

The next leg of our journey took us to Santa Clara. We traveled in a 1949 school bus through Cuban countryside and were able to see firsthand pineapple and sugar cane fields, coconut groves and beef cattle grazing. Cuba is one of the world leaders in sustainable agriculture. In Santa Clara, we did some painting at a small church and were able to talk with a 94-year-old goatherd whose animals "mowed" the church lawn regularly. We ate black beans and rice, pork and plantain chips for lunch followed by a dessert of pralines sold to us by a vendor passing by the church. A decisive battle for the Revolution was fought in Santa Clara and it is there where the major tribute to Ernesto "Che" Guevara is housed, though his picture is everywhere along with Jose Marti, the Father of Cuban Independence, we did not see any statues or pictures of President Castro. There is a statue of Che at a museum dedicated to him and also a chapel containing an eternal flame in his honor and in honor of the soldiers who died in the revolution. This tribute to Che and the Revolution is sacred to Cubans and there are no souvenir stands to "cash in" on Guevara's world-wide fame.

All too soon I was back on the plane headed for Miami. The words of **Fernan Sanchez** echoed in my head as we flew over the lush Cuban countryside:

"Beautiful is the sugarcane, but even more your voice
which chases all bitterness from the heart & as I gaze upon you,
my lute sighs,
blessing you, my unparalled beauty
because you are Cuba."

An Ever-Present Storm

Henry laughed darkly, or so his wife thought, at the ferocity of her orderliness. Marion conceded that she did make lists and that she also checked off each task as it was done: dishes washed, beds made, daily walk accomplished and so on. She realized that her sense of purpose amused her husband, and his amusement irritated her. To her, it seemed Henry only cared that meals were ready on time and that she let him alone to read his papers and watch the many news shows he enjoyed on television.

Still, she reasoned, they were often both awestruck by the same piece of music, a full moon or the soft scent of lilac on a spring day. The truth was that these kinds of moments came often in their life together.

Nevertheless, since the day they met, there seemed to be something like thunder in the distance announcing an ever-present storm. Marion would never forget the weekend they met though it had been more than forty years ago. It seemed to her as though the storms in that long ago spring must have originated in some primeval place. Gods and goddesses, she thought, must have directed the thunder, lightning and rain from some far away realm. Those storms were so awesome and relentless that people still spoke of them.

"Did you read the editorial page today?" Henry asked his wife.

They sat across from each other at the kitchen table eating breakfast. Hers was orange juice, toast and coffee and his was bacon, eggs, toast and juice. She felt anger at the hereditary force which made her cholesterol high and his well within a normal range. It was she, after all, who walked each day and carefully watched her diet. He only played golf a few months a year and ate whatever he pleased.

"No," she said. "I haven't had a chance to look at the paper. Is there something today that stands out?" she asked.

"There's a commentary by a local boy about Langston Hughes that I think you might find interesting," he answered.

"I'll look for it," Marion said. "What does he say?"

"Well, I can't explain it, but he writes about how Langston's writing has influenced people's speech whether they've read him or not. I can't express it that well. You ought to read it for yourself. I think you'll like it."

"I will," Marion said. "Then we can discuss it." She felt a swell of love for him, even as she watched him finish off the last bit of bacon.

The remainder of her morning was spent tidying their home—washing dishes, making up the bed they shared and putting this, that and the other thing in place.

Mid-morning Henry kissed her goodbye and left to spend a few hours filling grocery orders for seniors at their community's food shelf. Marion showered and changed her clothes to ready herself for a luncheon date with women friends.

She met them at a neighborhood restaurant called Maria's that specialized in Mexican food. Marion enjoyed visiting the growing number of ethnic restaurants that had seemed to spring up over the past couple of years. She and her friends exchanged conversation about recent books they had read and updated each other on children and grandchildren.

Marion declined the offer of a ride home, preferring to use this opportunity to get in her daily walk. The several blocks to and from the restaurant, she deduced, would serve to make up the mile she had vowed to walk five or six days a week.

Upon her return home, she found Henry asleep in his chair in front of the television, remote control in hand and newspaper on the floor.

Marion gently took the remote from his hand to lower the volume. She did not turn the television off, fearing the sudden silence would wake him. He slept poorly many nights so she did not want to disturb his rest. He chose to be so mentally involved with the world and was often troubled that it so often seemed headed for disaster. She kissed his forehead lightly, put the newspaper in order and went upstairs to work on the newsletter she edited every other month for her church.

Lent would begin soon, so much of the copy involved announcements for special services and study opportunities for different age groups. The rector had written an interesting piece on various ways people kept Lent during various historical periods. Though Henry wasn't a church-going man, she knew he would find the article interesting and decided to share it with him later.

The telephone rang. Though in the midst of her editing, Marion answered immediately so the ringing would not wake her husband.

"Hello."

"Hi, Mom," her daughter said. "Did Dad tell you I called?"

"No. He is taking a nap, so I haven't actually spoken to him since I got back."

"That's okay. I just called to see if you and Dad would like to see the Timberwolves play on Friday night."

"Well," Marion said, "You know I'm not really a fan, but Dad would like it so, sure, I'm game."

"Ray and I thought," her daughter continued, "that we could have an early dinner first. What do you think?"

"That sounds fine, but I would like to make sure Dad is up for this before I give you a definite answer or did you already ask him?"

"No." Karne laughed. "I know you handle the 'social calendar', so I thought I should talk with you. When will I hear from you?"

"Tonight. I'll let you know tonight."

Their daughter, Karne, worked for an advertising agency doing graphic design. Her husband, Ray was in Human Resources at the same company. It was there they had met. Marion thought they were a lovely couple and their working arrangement was nearly perfect. They could ride to work together and still each have the space to pursue separate careers. Neither wanted children, and though Henry was suspicious about their reasons, they both seemed very happy.

"Who was that on the phone," Henry called to his wife.

"It was Karne," she answered. "Let me finish what I'm doing and then I'll come down and we can talk."

"Okay. She called for while you were out," he answered. "Nothing is wrong, is it?"

"No. Everything is fine."

Marion completed her editing task and placed the corrected pages in an envelope. She would drop the newsletter by her church during her morning walk tomorrow.

When she arrived downstairs, Henry was in the kitchen making tea. "Do you want some tea?" he asked.

"Yes," she said. "That would be lovely."

"What's on Karne's mind?" Henry asked her.

"She and Ray have invited us to a Timberwolves game on Friday and they want us to have dinner with them first. I told her I would let them know after I discussed it with you."

"Do you want to go?" Henry asked his wife.

"Sounds like fun," she said.

"But you don't much like basketball," he protested.

"I know. But spending the evening as a family sounds nice. What we do doesn't seem so important. We'll be together. That's what counts."

"I'm surprised they asked us."

"Why?"

"We hardly ever see them. They're always so damned busy working or entertaining their fancy white friends. I thought Karne had pretty much written us off, or at least her old man. I suppose you don't embarrass her quite as much as I do."

Marion pushed her chair back and got up to rinse her cup. "Why," she said, "do you always have to say such ugly things? Karne has never once said or done anything to give you any reason to think the way you do." She turned from the sink to look at him. "And," she continued, "neither has Ray, nor, for that matter, have his parents. They are perfectly lovely people and treat Karne just fine. Why must you always look for the worst in people?" By now Marion had tears in her eyes.

"I'll let her know that you don't want to go." She sat down again at the kitchen table and sat staring at Henry. "What the hell is wrong with you?" She asked him.

"Well," he said, "when you've been around as long as I have, you can just sort of feel when things aren't right, and I think our daughter has come to believe she's white."

"Why shouldn't she?" Marion said, standing up and leaning across the table towards her husband. "Isn't she as much white as she is black?"

"And what do you think Ray's parents see?" Henry replied. "You can bet it's not a white girl and dark as I am, I think Karne just sees me as a reminder of who she really is."

"You are behaving like it's still 1950. We're in the new millennium for God's sake. Some things have gotten better, and despite what you seem to think, being white and being a racist are not necessarily the same thing. How can you even be with me, thinking as you do?" Frustrated, Marion turned and walked out of the room.

In her heart she knew Henry didn't believe the things he said. He spoke from fear and from the experiences of his own youth and early manhood. It was so hard for him to accept that his son-in-law loved their daughter and that his parents accepted Karne as his wife. Marion supposed it was the way he chose to keep from being hurt or disappointed. She also knew that eventually, maybe even later today, he would change his mind and agree to accept the invitation extended by their daughter and her husband.

"I should be used to this by now," Marion thought and felt angry at having let herself be drawn into the conversation. She knew there was no reasonable argument she could put forth to combat the depth of his hurt. Most of the time, she was able to just listen, knowing what her husband said and felt had nothing to do with her. But there were times, like today, when she couldn't hold her tongue.

She went upstairs to their room and lay on the bed for a few minutes, thinking a nap might leave her feeling refreshed. But, she couldn't sleep. She got up and went to the bathroom and splashed some water on her face. As she looked at her reflection in the mirror, Marion noted how the anger in her heart affected her looks. She put on some lipstick and went downstairs to the hall closet to get her coat.

"I need to get out of the house for a while," she announced to Henry as she headed for the back door. "I'm going next door. I won't be long."

"Say 'hello' to Dale," Henry said.

Looking over her shoulder, Marion answered, "I will."

"Henry walked up behind her and grabbed her arm. "Don't I get a kiss goodbye?" he asked her. Marion gave him a quick kiss on the lips and continued on her way.

When she reached her neighbor's house, he had just made a pot of fresh coffee. "This will be a real treat," Dale said. "It's a special blend I just created. Tell me what you think."

She sat down at the table as he poured the special brew into fragile china cups. He brought out some cookies, imported from Belgium. "You look as though you could use a special treat," he said to Marion.

"I'm not supposed to…"

Dale interrupted her. "I know. Your cholesterol. Just eat one. Live a little. Don't be so rigid."

"Am I that bad?" Marion asked.

"Sometimes, beautiful lady, you're a real pain in the ass," Dale told her.

Marion laughed. "You're right," she agreed and reached for a cookie.

"Alright. Tell me. What did he do this time?" Dale asked.

"How did you know?" Marion asked him.

"You're not very good at hiding your feelings," Dale told her. "Isn't that why you came over; to get out of the house and away from Henry's god-awful negativity?"

"Dale, stop. You make him sound like some horrible, ugly person and you know as well as I that he isn't that at all."

"Okay. I forgot. Rules are that you are the only one who can ever be critical of your husband. Now, tell me what he did."

"It was about Karne and Ray," Marion explained. "They invited us to dinner and a basketball game and Henry went into one of his rants about Karne thinking she's white."

"Oh, my God! What did she say?"

"No, no. She wasn't there. She telephoned me with the invitation and Henry started in on her when I asked him if he wanted to go."

"Well, thank God she didn't hear it because a sweeter, more thoughtful daughter never lived," Dale reasoned.

"I know," Marion agreed.

"Anyway we both know this is about Henry and not about Karne." Dale reached across the table and took Marion's hand. "And," he continued, "it's not about you either."

Marion nodded her head in agreement. Dale always helped her put things in perspective. "You're right, of course," she said. "And before the day is over, he'll be sorry, apologize and everything will be fine again. I shouldn't have let it get to me."

"You're not a saint, my dear, and that's what I'm here for," Dale patted her hand.

"You know you're the dearest friend I have," Marion told Dale.

"Yes, yes. I know. Now let's talk about something else. I just have to tell you about the event I'm planning at the club."

Dale worked at a rather glamorous nightclub and events center in the theater district as an event planner. It was a place where politicians and charitable organizations held fundraisers and, though retired now, when something especially important was in the works, Dale was called upon to assist.

The event he told Marion about was a fundraiser for the local Habitat for Humanity branch and, it seemed a certain ex-president from Georgia was scheduled to make an appearance. Dale complained about Secret Service officers' demands, but was generally very excited to be involved. "I can get you and Henry tickets, if you want," he offered.

"Now that would be something I know Henry would love," Marion said.

"And what about you?" Dale asked. "You have to get a new dress, your nails done and I'll get you and appointment with Carl for your hair. President Jimmy will be lusting in his heart all over again."

They both laughed. Marion looked at her watch. "I should start dinner," she said.

"Alright. I'll let you know about the Habitat event. It's a month away, so plan to buy something summery to wear. I can't wait to see what you find. You know I love your taste in clothes," Dale told her.

Marion thanked Dale for his support, friendship and the cookie and coffee. "You're always here for me too," he said, "and so is Henry." They hugged each other and Marion left to return to her home.

When she entered their kitchen, Henry was already preparing dinner.

"What's this? She asked. Henry normally only cooked on weekends or when they were expecting guests.

"We're having steak, greens, baked sweet potatoes and biscuits," he said.

"A peace offering?" Marion asked.

I suppose you could call it that." He pulled her close to him. "I'm pretty rough on you sometimes," he said, "and you deserve better."

"I'll set the table," she said.

"Let's eat in the dining room tonight," he said, "and light some candles."

"You mean we're not going to eat in front of the TV tonight?" Marion smiled.

"Like you said, this is a peace offering."

Eating in front of the television was something Marion deplored, but Henry liked it and so after Karne was out on her own, she had given in. It was one of those things that just didn't seem important enough to disagree on any more.

Following Henry's lead, Marion set the table with their best china and chose a Clifford Brown CD for dinner music. Henry would be pleased because Brown was his favorite trumpet player.

She went upstairs to refresh her lipstick and when she returned, Henry was already placing serving dishes on the table. Marion lit the candles and turned on the CD player. Henry pulled out her chair and kissed her hair. They bowed their heads while Marion said the table grace.

"This is really good," Marion said after tasting her steak.

"I thought you'd like it. I used a different marinade, but I think this is just some good steak, so there probably isn't much I could have done to mess it up," Henry offered. They both laughed.

"I was thinking about when Karne was doing her internship with that theater group. Do you remember?" Henry asked his wife.

"Yes. I do. She really enjoyed that. She made friends who she still sees," Marion recalled.

"What was that black girl's name?" Henry asked.

"Tammy," Marion answered. "She and her husband see quite a bit of Karne and Ray."

"Is her old man white too?" Henry asked.

"Oh no," thought Marion. "Here we go again."

"No," Marion answered. "Her husband is black. He's a stockbroker or something. Anyway, I know he works for some investment firm."

"Anyway," Henry continued, "we went to a lot of plays at that theater while Karne was there didn't we?"

"Yes," Marion replied. "I think we saw every one she designed sets for. Remember how beautiful the ones were that she did for *Midsummer Night's Dream?*"

"She liked it that we came," Henry recalled. "She even invited us to one of the cast parties. Do you remember?"

"Yes. I do. Those were good times," Marion said.

"Our daughter has turned out to be a fine woman," Henry said, more to himself than to his wife. Marion remained silent.

Finally she said, "I'll clear up the dishes. You go on in and watch television."

"Before I turn on the TV, I think I'll call Karne and Ray to let them know we'll go to dinner and the game with them. You do still want to go, don't you?" he asked his wife.

Marion smiled, "Yes," she said. "I'm looking forward to it." She began to stack the dishes.

"Hey!" Henry said. Marion looked at him.

"Thanks for putting up with me," he said.

"I love you too," his wife responded. "Now, go call our daughter."

Returning to the kitchen, Marion noticed it was raining. Looking out the back window, she saw a flash of lightening and though she knew it was coming, the clap of thunder that followed startled her. She moved to the sink and readied the dishwater. "Maybe," she thought, "this will be a spring of thunderstorms like the ones we had the year Henry and I met." That year, she decided, was a very good year.

Spirits of New Orleans

I walk
in New Orleans
From St. Louis Cemetery #1
down
Rue St. Ann
towards the Mississippi River
through
the French Quarter
(wrapped in friendly fog).
The Spirits of the City:
King Oliver, Louis Armstrong, Pere Antoine, Professor Longhair
walk with me and
Indian spirits of the Choctaw & Chickasaw;
French, Spanish, Italian, German, African spirits.
The spirit of
Madame Marie LeVeau
kneels beside me in prayer at St. Louis Cathedral.
The Seven Powers of Africa
surround Jesus, Mary and Joseph.
"Laissez les bon temps retourne," she whispers to me.
"Oui," I reply
and repeat the phrase as a prayer.
The spirits rise with me and we walk
across Jackson Square where
the spirits

of General Andrew Jackson
(and Captain Jean Lafitte")
join us.
A Cajun fortune teller tips his hat and says,
"Bonjour Messieurs-dames,"
"Bonjour Monsieur," we reply.
Finally, the Spirits of New Orleans sit with me at
Café Du Monde—Café of the World.
We eat beignets and sip coffee laced with chicory.
We weep
for the broken heart
of the Crescent City.

Sermon

Arise, Sister Woman;
Awaken, Brother Man.
It's time to start liven'
by Father God's plan.

Open up the window;
let the wind in.
Stop drinkin' and gamblin';
stop liven' in sin.

Live by the moon
like the old folks did.
Tell the stories of your mommas and papas
to them sweet little kids.

Leave that whiskey
up on the shelf.
Be sweet to your woman or your man
and be good to your self.

Walk soft
on this garden called Earth;
give thanks to her soil
that gave you birth.

Arise, Sister Woman;
Awaken, Brother Man.
Start liven' today by
Father God's plan.

Can I have
an Amen!